THE KINGS AND QUEENS OF ENGLAND

A History In Verse

by Samuel Norman

Illustrated by Maria Smedstad

Published by Britannic Verses

Copyright © Samuel Norman, 2013

All rights reserved

Printed and bound by Tyson Press

ISBN 978-0-9927165-0-9

With many thanks to Glenn Rogers for the proofreading.

Foreword

The ghosts of forty kings and queens have kindly spared the time

To tell us who they were, and briefly set their reigns to rhyme.

With ever-raw emotion and a candour that is rare

Their triumphs and their tragedies Their Majesties will share.

They'll tell us how in different ways they shaped the land anew,

And how the strange experience of kingship shaped them too.

So please enjoy their better rhymes, and please forgive their worst,

Then in our nation's history you'll feel yourself well versed.

Contents

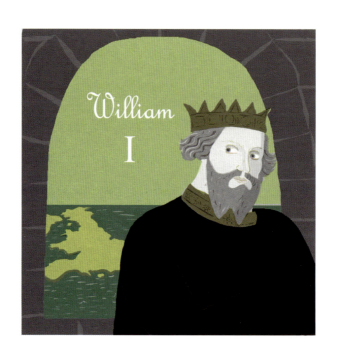

William

I

William I

(1066–1087)

As Duke of Normandy, I longed for England and her throne;
The England that my Viking kinsmen couldn't leave alone.
When Edward the Confessor died I armed my fiercest men,
Aware that such a chance as this would never come again.
Near York there fought two would-be kings who shared a Christian name;
At Hastings I prepared to fight whichever Harold came.
The Saxon Harold Godwinson took on our Norman might.
The day was ours and Harold's last; his men alive took flight.
Invasion wasn't all; I had to conquer inch by inch.
Though gruesome tasks would bloody me, I knew I must not flinch.
I scorched the earth, and then I sowed the seats of Norman power:
The castles and cathedrals which would make the natives cower.
Two thousand dreadful days the conquest took; but this appears
A good investment, now my sons have reigned a thousand years.
A horse it was that finished me; in fright it bucked and flailed,
Unseating me, succeeding where the Saxon race had failed.

3

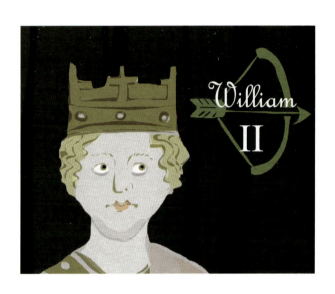

William II

(1087–1100)

The Conqueror decided that the Duchy and the Realm
Should have no single member of his offspring at the helm.
For Robert, Normandy; for me the chilly English throne,
Its subjects keen to make their anti-Norman feelings known.
My barons were dismayed by the imperial divide;
It took diverse persuasive arts to get them on my side.
Then Malcolm Canmore, murderer of murderous Macbeth,
Came down in rage from Scotland; Northern England held its breath.
Proud son of England's conqueror, I'd bear no conquest's shame.
The year ten ninety-one, I sent him back from whence he came.
My brother fought a long crusade; the cost was borne by me,
But in exchange I took control of Robert's Normandy.
Out hunting was my favourite way to spend an idle day,
But finally in my New Forest, hunting, I fell prey.
I'd like to think the arrow was in search of boar or deer,
But kings are rarely slain by simple accident, I fear.

Henry I

Henry I
(1100–1135)

As fourth son of the Conqueror, my reign was not foreseen,

But when the opportunity arose, it found me keen.

My brother Robert, England's heir, off waging Holy Wars,

Would take some weeks or months to journey back to England's shores.

Meanwhile back here the situation worsened hour by hour,

For criminality adores a state bereft of power.

I vaunted all my virtues; my ambition I made clear.

The argument that seemed to clinch the deal was, "I am here."

At Alton, Hampshire, Robert came and saw I'd got my way.

I then invaded Normandy, and won at Tinchebray.

Now England controlled Normandy, the greater land the lesser;

The whale had swallowed back the fish; possessed was now possessor.

My long reign's blackest day was when the White Ship ran aground;

My son, lone hope of Norman continuity, was drowned.

As heir I named Matilda, living daughter for dead son,

And hoped no upstart would usurp the throne, as I had done.

Stephen

Stephen
(1135–1154)

The barons didn't want a monarch of Matilda's sex,

So spurned her as *Regina* and invested me as *Rex*.

They crowned me on midwinter's day, hands shivering and numb;

The crown came down reluctantly, and didn't quite land plum.

At Arundel in Sussex in eleven thirty-nine

Matilda tried to pinch the crown, but victory was mine.

An England gripped by civil war those Scotsmen preyed upon:

Northumberland and Cumberland and Westmorland, all gone;

Although the barons seemed to have a weakness for my charm,

My weakness disenchanted them; they also chose to arm.

But when she came to claim the crown, my foe was forced to flee;

Matilda was (God bless her) even more disliked than me.

My son named Eustace died before me — such a bitter blow,

But maybe this saved poor Anarchic England further woe.

Matilda's son would now succeed, once I had found my tomb;

I'd stopped the woman's head from being crowned, but not her womb.

Henry

II

Henry II
(1154–1189)

The first Plantagenet, my reign saw England reawaken.
I soon claimed back the northern counties Stephen had forsaken.
A power struggle raged between the Mitre and the Crown,
With Thomas Becket doing all he could to bring me down.
Although I wanted Becket gone, I'd never wished him dead,
But Canterbury Cathedral's stony floor was stained blood-red.
On Eleanor of Aquitaine, my Queen, the barons fawned;
For thanks to her upon the court chivalric culture dawned.
To my extensive lands was knitted Eleanor's domain,
Which left me lord of everything from Scotland down to Spain.
My wife and I fought tooth and nail, but must have sometimes truced;
How else, I ask you, could eight bouncing babies be produced?
I loved my sons, but they rebelled and caused such bitter strife,
At times I came to rue my choice of such a fertile wife.
Though all kings face antipathy, my case is sad to hear:
No subjects held their king more cheap than those he held most dear.

Richard

I

Richard I

(1189–1199)

The Lionheart was I, of brave and glorious renown.
I cared more for my sword than for an ornamental crown.
Once King I went crusading, full of hope and Christian pride,
Eyes eastward, leaving England far behind, a jilted bride.
I captured Cyprus, Acre and Arsuf; while proud of them,
I grew frustrated when we failed to take Jerusalem.
Some allies then deserted; I accused them of betrayal.
Offending Europe's kings and princes landed me in jail.
I wasn't meant to be confined; I greatly pined away,
Composing songs of love and war waged in a kinder way.
In taxes England raised the sum required to set me free:
A quarter of her gold purchased a rusty iron key.
Poor England, I neglected her; this was my greatest crime.
On me she spent her riches, but for her I spared no time.
Yet Nature can't be fought; my every sinew, every bone
Implored me: "Roam and conquer — don't sit idle on a throne."

John

Magna Carta

John
(1199–1216)

Incompetent and ruthless, I disgraced the English throne.
I plagued my father's and my brother's reigns, then plagued my own.

I had a rival in my nephew; many backed his claim.
His face was young and innocent, and Arthur was his name.

I had the lad imprisoned by my most obliging men;
I won't say what befell him, but he wasn't seen again.

I quarrelled with the Pope, and then was banished from the fold;
My subjects weren't impressed to have their worship put on hold.

The barons wrote a document for all the world to see,
Enshrining civil liberties, and taking power from me.

A rule book binding me and every monarch to succeed
Was Magna Carta, signed in twelve fifteen at Runnymede.

I lost the crown of England to the Wash's tidal swell.
To prove my carelessness I lost our French domains as well.

The merit of my kingship's rather hard to ascertain,
If not to show all future kings and queens how not to reign.

15

Henry III
(1216–1272)

My father, hapless John, passed on when I was was yet unschooled;

While I was taught the perils of my birth-right, regents ruled.

The splendid William Marshal got the barons on my side

By promising that Magna Carta's laws would be applied.

He also beat the French as they attempted to invade,

So all our fears for England, for the meantime, were allayed.

But when I came to power I invited my French cousins

To join me at the English court: not just a couple — dozens;

The barons were appalled by all these Guillaumes and Pierres

Acquiring lands and titles which they felt by rights were theirs.

Simon de Montfort in the end saw cause to break the peace.

He wanted Parliament to rule the land, not my caprice.

At Lewes Simon won the day, and I was overthrown.

My dear son Edward, though, put me back safely on the throne.

From vain kings' tyranny the land had started to break free,

And journey down the tricky road towards democracy.

17

Edward

I

Edward I

(1272–1307)

The Hammer of the Scots, *Scottorum Malleus*, was I;

Percussion is the way to make one's enemies comply.

It took a while but in the end the Scots were dispossessed;

Robert the Bruce and William Wallace came off second best.

And Wales, too, experienced my subjugating spree;

Land of my fathers it was not; land of my sons, maybe.

I built a ring of castles there to clarify my will,

And made my son the Prince of Wales — a custom honoured still.

My wife and I lived happily, until that idyll burst;

O Eleanor, dear Eleanor, O how could you die first?

Twelve crosses I had made so men might offer her a prayer,

So people would remember her, twelve spikes of my despair.

I hired the finest masons so these monuments might be

As lovely and as graceful — just more durable than she.

The Hammer of the Scots I am, but truly I prefer

The hammer of the chisel of these monuments to her.

Edward II

Edward II
(1307–1327)

My torrid reign's the one in which the scandal-hunter delves.
It's full of passion, cruelty and vice, so brace yourselves.
Strikingly handsome, clever, I was of my era; yet
My vain approach to kingship was far less Plantagenet.
The love I bore Piers Gaveston caused many to object;
My barons and my wife bore ill their sovereign's neglect.
The barons, jealous of my favour, wanted Piers gone,
And so they killed him brutally. I reeled, but I reigned on.
My wife, Queen Isabella, was embarrassed by the sneers
And smirks around the court when other knights succeeded Piers.
To vengeance of a woman scorned kings sadly aren't immune.
I'd sung to her a chilly air; she howled me back typhoon.
To visit her French kinsmen she was easily persuaded.
Then she and her new lover, Roger Mortimer, invaded.
Imprisoned, tortured, killed I was by dear old Isabella,
Which left the kingless kingdom ruled by her, and her new feller.

21

Edward

Edward III

(1327–1377)

My reign is one on which the English fondly reminisce,
And not one that the French recall with undiluted bliss.
I first disposed of Mortimer; he'd earned a traitor's fate.
My mother begged me not to — far too little, far too late.
As grandson of the late French King, I advertised my line,
Aware that crowns were often won with far worse claims than mine.
The French attacked my Aquitaine, which I could not ignore;
I soon struck back, and so commenced a Hundred Years of War.
At Crécy I saw victory in thirteen forty-six,
Our archers raining down on them a deadly shower of sticks.
We then took Calais, in what proved to be a lengthy stay.
My son, the great Black Prince, won handsomely at Poitiers.
Against the Scots, York's brave Archbishop led an army forth,
And won at Neville's Cross to stop them ravaging the North.
My fifty-year-long reign saw barons' private quarrels cease —
There's nothing like incessant war to guarantee the peace.

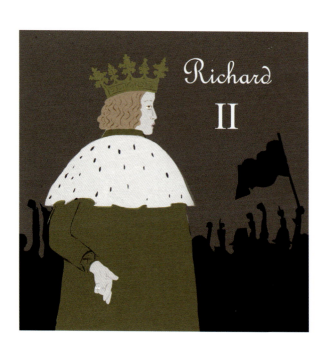

Richard II

Richard II
(1377–1399)

I found myself enthroned too young to play a sovereign's role,

So John of Gaunt, the Duke of Lancaster, first took control.

To pay for wars in France where English victories were lean,

I introduced a poll tax, but the peasants weren't that keen.

From far and wide they marched to London, in defiant mood;

They hoped their king would set them free from life-long servitude.

At Smithfield they confronted me, a vast and hostile sea.

Aged just fourteen I told them they'd be led by only me.

They cheered as I said: "Liberty you justly shall obtain,"

But, when they'd gone, said: "Serfs you are, and serfs you shall remain."

When John of Gaunt's old heart fell still, I didn't quite play fair:

I seized his huge estates from Henry Bolingbroke, his heir.

But Bolingbroke struck back, and as his vengeful army neared,

My friends, who smelled the downfall of a tyrant, disappeared.

He had me jailed and killed — though this was not quite by the book,

My greed and guile were such that I deserved a Bolingbroke.

25

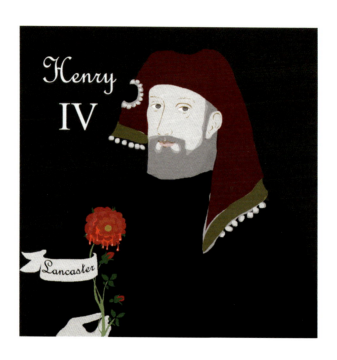

Henry IV

Lancaster

Henry IV
(1399–1413)

The rose of Lancaster, from which three English kings would bud,

Had petals that were crimson, as if steeped in Richard's blood;

And I, the first Lancastrian to reign, felt constant dread

That Richard's ghost would track me down, or — worse — he wasn't dead.

Once King I faced hostility, which seemed to me insane,

From those who'd helped me put an end to Richard's life and reign.

They felt King Henry wasn't like the Bolingbroke they'd known,

And terrorised a monarch not yet settled on his throne.

The treachery of Henry Percy could not be concealed;

I killed young Hotspur, Percy's son, on Shrewsbury's battlefield.

The Welshman Owen Glendower kept England on her toes,

And how I came to quash his proud Welsh army, heaven knows.

Rebellion led to death for York's Archbishop, Richard Scrope,

Which got me into trouble with my people and the Pope.

I fought my constant enemies, I fought my friends disloyal,

To keep the crown for sons of mine, and keep the red rose royal.

27

Henry
V

Henry V
(1413–1422)

At home on muddy battlefields, I fought with strength and grace;

At Shrewsbury though a Welshman's arrow scarred my teenage face.

Thank God, for some beholders in a blemish beauty lies:

When soldiers saw my scar I saw devotion in their eyes.

The French had backed the Welsh against us — time we two should meet.

If France would have us beaten, she would have to risk defeat.

I made some gains in northern France which didn't come with ease,

For half our loyal men were lost to battle or disease.

Depleted and fatigued, we met the French at Agincourt,

Both armies deadly keen to end our Hundred Years of War.

"To stay alive, men, fight," I said, "and fight for England too."

They did their job, and France succumbed to England's weary few.

Before the French King's daughter I got down on bended knee,

And soon a treaty signed at Troyes accorded France to me.

I never left the battlefield, where pestilence was rife,

And there succumbed before my time; I'd bought France with my life.

Henry VI

Henry VI
(1422–1461, 1470–1471)

When I was King, between two royal Houses trouble stirred.
The quarrel started with the sons of Edward Rex the third.

The line of the Plantagenets had there become a fork,
With John of Gaunt's side Lancaster, and Edmund Langley's York.
Although we sons of Lancaster had made our weak claim good,

I couldn't stand the battlefield, where tall my fathers stood.
The gentlemen of Lancaster fought Yorkists rough and wild;
The battle done, they'd find me somewhere, singing like a child.
An Act was passed in Parliament that backed the Yorkist claim.

My rival, Richard, Duke of York, then almost won the game.
At Wakefield, though, my gentlemen relieved him of his head.
The Earl of March, his son, took on the Yorkist cause instead.

The Yorkists had me put in prison where they hoped I'd rot.
My son, Prince Edward, fought for me; I wish that he had not.
At Tewkesbury Edward met his death and then, when I met mine,

No blood of Lancaster remained to paint our royal line.

31

Edward

IV

Edward IV
(1461–1470, 1471–1483)

As Earl of March, my hard-won battles spelled King Henry's doom,

And thereby set the rose of York in snow-white royal bloom.

At Towton was the toughest fight. I grimly made the cry:

"Cut down those proud Lancastrians; go kill for York, or die."

The sky snowed blood and men bled snow, if we believed our sight,

And Nature's palette only had two colours: red and white.

No battle ever poured more blood on England's fertile earth,

For thirty thousand men that day was what the crown was worth.

My ally, Warwick, took against Elizabeth, my bride,

And in the raging civil war, he joined the other side.

The battle fought at Barnet brought about his own decease,

And after Tewkesbury all was well, and I could reign in peace.

I saw the future bright: "More Yorkist Edwards there will be;

Lancastrian King Henrys just a distant memory.

My sons, if I should die, you'll be protected by my brother;

What perils lurk about this court for you, boys, he will smother."

33

Edward V

Edward V

(1483)

"Oh brother, there are men who would usurp our royal power,

And that is why our Uncle Richard's locked us in the Tower.

I hate to be here too, for it is cold and it is grim,

But Uncle Richard says we must, and we must trust in him.

Don't cry, dear brother, please don't cry; we shan't be here life-long,

For we shall overpower the guards when we are big and strong,

And once the people put me back upon my father's throne,

I'll prove as fine and just a king as England's ever known.

But brother, who is this, whose footsteps echo stonily?

They must be sent from Richard, for the lock admits their key.

Good day, dear sir, or is it night? This chamber starves the eye;

We don't know here if sun or moon is sovereign of the sky.

You offer neither word nor bow, but slow towards us creep,

A pillow in your hands to help us pining princes sleep...

Stand back, assassin! Hear your king! Now brother, you must cry:

Remind our sleeping kingdom that we live, or else we die!"

35

Richard

III

36

Richard III
(1483–1485)

In youth, the cause I fought for was my brother's, not my own:
At Barnet and at Tewkesbury, I fixed Edward's rocky throne.
The bride of Lancaster's young heir, the Earl of Warwick's daughter,
Bewitched me, and by chance her husband fell at Tewkesbury's slaughter.

This Anne, no partisan, an either party's Anne in war,
Then loved her husband's enemy, once he could love no more.
When brother Edward's time was up, I turned a trifle mean,
And questioned whether he was rightly married to his Queen,
And whether the gold hoop should land upon the Queen's first son,
Or Edward's younger brother; that is how my crown was won.
The Tower of London's where the sons of Edward were confined.
They found, like many others since, the exit hard to find.
I died at Bosworth Field, an honest soldier at his post;
To die among his troops can claim no younger royal ghost.
Young Henry Tudor and his army felled, in felling me,
Not just the branch of York, but the entire Plantagenet tree.

Henry
VII

38

Henry VII
(1485–1509)

The Roses' Wars had seen too many hats thrown in the ring:

Too many royal families each offering a king.

The Percy sons and Neville lads, alas, for all their noise,

Would not attain the glory of us quiet Tudor boys.

My Welsh paternal grandfather made good at Agincourt;

The widow of the fifth King Henry made him Tudors more.

But it was to my mother that my royalty was owed,

For through the veins of Margaret Beaufort John of Gaunt's blood flowed.

I won the crown at Bosworth Field in fourteen eighty-five.

The Tudor era had begun; how long would it survive?

I thought it best to marry someone from the other side:

Elizabeth of York I took at once to be my bride.

To show that York and Lancaster were now conciliated,

The Tudor Rose was born, of red and white cross-pollinated.

And there's no doubt our marriage was a blessing for the state;

A love of two to pacify a countryful of hate.

Henry VIII

Henry VIII
(1509–1547)

My royal journey started when my elder brother died.

I quickly married Catherine of Aragon, his bride,

But wished to end the marriage when she bore no son and heir;

The future of the realm was surely worth a queen's despair.

The Pope said: "Check the Bible. That'll tell you if you may":

Though Deuteronomy said 'aye', Leviticus said 'nay'.

Rome's Pope and England's church I knew I'd have to disentwine;

If that divorce did not take place, I'd not be granted mine.

I made myself the church's head, and London the new Rome.

To make a mother of a son I now was free to roam.

A monarch fully fledged I stood magnificently preened,

And every female near me ran the risk of being queened.

My half a dozen wives, more fun to chase than to retain,

Consisted of three Catherines, two Annes and one fair Jane.

Alas, despite my manful efforts with this queenly lot,

And all their labours, just one princeling warmed the Tudor cot.

41

Edward

VI

Edward VI
(1547–1553)

Three children of three mothers grew while Henry reigned on high:

The two princesses, Mary and Elizabeth, and I.

Of strange and troubled childhoods we siblings bore the scars,

But learned to love our father, and speak not of our mamas.

A sober child, I did not share the late king's bonhomie;

To gazing on men's faces I preferred astronomy.

The throne, all warped from where the giant Henry used to sit,

For my young slender cargo was a somewhat looser fit.

My mother's brother, Edward Seymour, protestant devout,

Was Lord Protector. Under his strict auspices rang out

The transcendental glories of the Book of Common Prayer;

May anyone who doubts that God speaks English look in there.

The Catholics and Protestants, like Godless tribes of yore,

Began a long and deadly feud: a Tudor civil war.

At fifteen years, I left my realm for where I now reside —

Another kingdom, where in peace we all live side by side.

43

Mary

I

Mary I
(1553–1558)

When Edward died, my royal tenure faced nine days' delay:
The interlude of Protestant pretender, young Jane Grey.
In order to ensure the crown she'd stolen would not fit,
I had her pretty head cut off — the surest way, to wit.
I knew within my soul what God had made me Sovereign for:
To make my poor misguided England Catholic once more.
I put in prison all the bishops from my brother's reign,
And then resolved to marry Philip, Prince of papist Spain.
In me he found a loving bride, but proved a heartless groom.
Despairing, I claimed pregnancy despite an empty womb.
Some rebels led by Thomas Wyatt challenged my direction,
And I could sense Elizabeth behind this insurrection.
Although I didn't hesitate to chop off Wyatt's head,
I had no proof against young Bess, so locked her up instead.
They called me 'Bloody Mary'; while it's true I spilled some gore,
My sister should be grateful I refrained from spilling more.

45

Elizabeth I

Elizabeth I

(1558–1603)

My sovereignty as Queen I knew a husband would deplete;

With no man at my side I could have all men at my feet.

I faced invasion by the King of Spain, my brother-in-law.

He'd wooed me once, and hadn't liked the answer: "No, señor."

Although I had the body of a weak and feeble thing,

I roused my troops and showed the heart and stomach of a king.

My proud and fearless navy and a rather useful breeze

Defeated Spain's Armada; I was mistress of the seas.

Sir Francis Drake and Walter Ralleigh for their queen unfurled

Their thirty-foot high sails and went in search of the new world.

My age gave Shakespeare — unlike mine, his power does not wane

For he is still the poet king. Long may my subject reign.

Now due to her involvement in some anti-English plots,

Against my will I killed my cousin, Mary Queen of Scots,

But when I had to name my heir, I said with dying breath:

"The son of Scotland's Mary shall succeed Elizabeth."

47

James

I

James I
(1603–1625)

My ancient, Stuart lineage was royal as can be;
A regal disposition, though, blue blood can't guarantee.
Though clever, I was silly — so much so, to my regret,
"The wisest fool in Christendom" became my epithet.
But questions of my kingliness received this sure reply:
"The choice of God no man on Earth should seek to justify."
Since childhood I was King of Scotland, then gained England's seat.
In me two ancient monarchies at last were forced to meet.
The parliaments of these two nations, enemies long sworn,
Would not allow the kingdom of Great Britain to be born,
So, two crowns on my head, I honed my balancing techniques,
While sitting on two thrones caused some discomfort for my cheeks.
My parliament at Westminster Guy Fawkes tried to ignite,
For which he dies a thousand deaths each year on bonfire night.
Invincible, I knew that such a plot would be exposed,
For God would never let a Stuart monarch be deposed.

49

Charles

I

Charles I
(1625–1649)

The grace of God had set me high; my downfall was self-made.

What divine right had given me, my human wrongs betrayed.

I tampered with our fragile Church; I taxed for private gain;

And Parliament for me was just an object of disdain.

We came to blows — a Civil War raged on for six long years.

The Roundheads fought for Parliament; for me, the Cavaliers.

In truth I didn't care that England suffered all the while,

Until at length the Roundheads won, and I was put on trial.

"For what offence," I asked, "have I been summoned to this court?"

"For treason — King against the state." A clever touch, I thought.

The verdict soon was reached, and more in disbelief than shock,

I learned I was to put my royal neck upon the block.

The day arrived. I prayed, and then, as all condemned men must,

Excused my executioner, knelt down, and bit the dust.

No king or queen ruled England now. Lord Cromwell filled the void,

And though the crown was melted down, the throne was not destroyed.

Charles II

Charles II
(1660–1685)

Lord Cromwell sat upon the seat my father once had known.

In vain I fought at Worcester to re-royalise the throne,

And famously avoided capture hiding up an oak.

At length, when Cromwell passed away, our monarchy awoke.

During my reign two Great Events had London gripped by fear:

The Plague in sixteen sixty-five, and Fire the following year.

With life so short, I held a merry, hedonistic court,

And didn't quite behave as England's foremost noble ought.

My courtiers were witty men, adept at repartee.

I didn't mind a jibe or two. Once this was said of me:

"He never said a foolish thing, and never did a wise one."

"My words are mine," said I, "One's deeds one's government denies one."

My artists and my scientists I fully got behind;

To learning, though, did not apply my sharp and able mind.

My gifts perhaps I wasted, but my father's final scenes

Had taught me — "Charles, live well within your intellectual means."

53

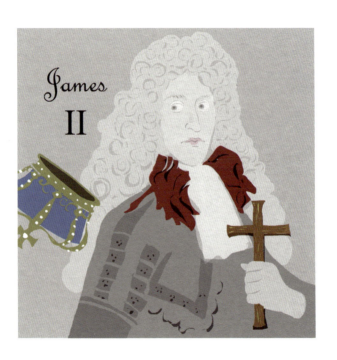

James

II

James II
(1685–1688)

A Catholic, a Duke of York, and then a King late-sworn

As Charles my brother fathered none (well, none his wife had borne).

The colony 'New Amsterdam' became 'New York' thenceforth,

Today a boggling namesake of my Duchy in the north.

Religion was my nemesis. Though warned, I paid no heed,

Conferring offices of state on those who shared my creed.

My daughters were raised Protestants, as was the late King's hope.

My second wife, however, was quite partial to the Pope.

A new-born son spelled trouble — he'd be Catholic like me.

A dynasty of Catholics was greatly feared, you see.

Dutch William of Orange and my daughter Mary wed.

"Invade us, and we'll welcome you," some English nobles said.

In sixteen eighty-eight the Dutch fleet made its bold advance.

I did not wish to fight and lose, and so I fled to France.

My line was disentitled, and the Stuart House brought down

By my robust resolve to put my creed before my crown.

55

William III and Mary II

(1688–1702 and 1688–1694)

Both: In one regard, our reign is England's most unusual yet —

Both: The opera of our Monarchy contains but one duet.

W: A grandson of King Charles the First, a Dutchman I had grown.

M: And I was James's daughter, therefore nearer to the throne.

W: My face was not a handsome one; you married me in tears.

M: Forgive a maiden's foolishness; my love grew with the years.

W: In sixteen eighty-eight my army landed in Torbay.

M: Invited by the Protestants, we came on Guy Fawkes' Day.

W: King James then fled the country so our armies never fought;

M: A Glorious Revolution of a very British sort.

W: I would not be the Consort of my wife, I would not deign…

M: …And I would not have wished you to. Together we would reign.

W: A Bill of Rights was drafted, curbing every royal vice.

M: The Government had chosen us. Obedience was the price.

Both: Our reign thus brought an end to selfish Stuart Monarchs' tricks,

Both: And also to the sovereign hopes of England's Catholics.

Anne

Anne
(1702–1714)

An elegant princess, of temper resolute but mild,
I gained the throne as William and Mary had no child,
And so it fell to George and me to make a Stuart heir.
The tally of our misery it grieves my heart to share:
Eight still-borns, four miscarriages, five dying in the cot;
Just one son reached eleven years, but twelve the lad did not.
In seventeen-o-seven my two kingdoms were undone;
The Scottish and the English crowns were fashioned into one:
Great Britain, proud inheritor of two great seats of kings,
With such exalted parent-realms, seemed destined for great things.
We warred with France as usual; great victories were ours
As we began our long campaign to balance Europe's powers.
John Churchill was the hero, wily foe of England's foes,
A man that makes a Queen think: "Subjects, breed me more of those."
My death then closed the chapter of the Stuarts' long demise:
At least our House had fallen with the kingdom on the rise.

59

George I
(1714–1727)

I ran over from Hanover to claim the great crown here.

Thus sprang the Georgian Age, of Georges *eins*, *zwei*, *drei* and *vier*.

My marriage to Sophia wasn't struck by Cupid's dart.

We had a son and daughter, but thereafter grew apart.

Like many kings I took a mistress — nothing there amiss!

Sophia had a lover too; I wasn't having this:

One summer's night this fellow was mysteriously slain.

I placed my wife on house arrest, there ever to remain.

My son George never felt again the kisses of his mother,

And in his eyes I saw we'd lost the love of one another.

He strove to lend opponents of my government support.

His house became a hotbed of dissent — a rival court.

The grand old squire of politics, Sir Robert Walpole, tried

To bring us back together, but the rift had grown too wide.

We Georges all had this in common — rancour multiplied

Between each father and his son, whom nothing should divide.

George

II

George II
(1727–1760)

My father was no pa to me; and I no son to him.
My coronation's joy the old king's passing would not dim:
What music! (Handel) Spectacle! (Baroque-Rococo style)
Poor God — He must have felt Himself out-gloried for a while.
The latest British king am I to lead his troops in war.
The fact I was victorious made people like me more.
In Europe and beyond the nation's hopes were all born out.
From ringing for these victories our church bells were worn out —
So many daring conquests and miraculous survivals
That thwarted the ambitions of our European rivals.
I had a son named Frederick, in many ways first-rate:
A cultured and a clever man, but object of my hate.
But his son, George, I looked on with affection and with pride,
And so much more when Frederick, at forty-three years, died.
My Queen and I did not lament this act of God above
Which meant the crown would skip a generation — like my love.

63

George

III

64

George III
(1760–1820)

A king of greater virtue, I, than many of my peers;

Of greater length of service too: I reigned for sixty years.

My subjects in America invited us to war.

The Spanish, French and Dutch all joined them — tricky, one v four.

At least their intervention made our hopeless struggle shorter.

America had left their king. I grieved, as for a daughter.

Elsewhere we gained in influence in spite of this mishap;

In India and Africa, and all across the map.

The Irish tamed, a new United Kingdom saw the day.

And at Trafalgar, Nelson kept Napoleon away.

A dreadful illness troubled me. With age it grew quite bad.

My doctors (who weren't up to much) just diagnosed me mad.

One day I chatted to an oak tree, which my mind construed

To be the King of Prussia, in a fairly quiet mood.

So colonies and sanity were chief amongst my losses,

But certainly my reign contained as many ticks as crosses.

George
IV

George IV
(1820–1830)

Extravagant and frivolous, committed bon viveur,

With gambling debts that no-one but a royal could incur;

A Prince that Britain, drained by war, grew tired of bailing out;

A Prince that Britain tutted at, but did nothing about,

All this was I: — Prince Regent when my father's health was poor

And after that as George the Fourth I reigned a decade more.

The fashion of my Regency was classical but new;

A well-proportioned elegance was everywhere in view.

I did my best to cultivate diverse artistic riches:

Jane Austen's novels; Haydn's tunes; Beau Brummel's shirts and breeches.

John Nash designed my Regent Street and also my Buck Pal.

I pushed for the creation of our treasured National Gal.

In age my belly, long abused, expanded to a size

No waistcoat with a bold cravat was able to disguise.

Of all my ailments, loneliness became my chief complaint,

As Fashionable Society had dropped its Patron Saint.

William

IV

William IV
(1830–1837)

Aged sixty-four I learned my brother, George the Fourth, was dead:
The British crown then found itself a much more level head.
Twelve years in Nelson's Navy had instilled in me the knack
Of taking orders graciously — what many princes lack.
At sea and on dry land I honed my easy-going style,
And learned how to be popular among the rank and file.
My seven-year-long innings saw one issue cause a storm:
The disenfranchised wanted parliamentary reform.
The Whig reformist government was headed by Lord Grey;
In parliament, polite debate soon turned into affray.
I raced to Westminster, where MPs' fists were poised like rockets.
I dissolved parliament. The clenched projectiles found their pockets.
Straight after an election, Grey's Reform Act was asserted,
Which gave more men the vote, and revolution was averted.
Alas, I had no children to replace me at the crease,
So after my departure came Victoria, my niece.

69

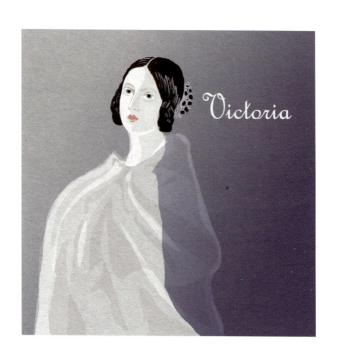

Victoria

Victoria

(1837–1901)

My domineering mother stripped my childhood of all joy:
No playmates, no adventures, no unsupervised employ.
One morning, asking for a private audience with me
Came the Lord Chamberlain and the Archbishop of Canterbury.
Mama, from just outside, asked what the secrecy was for.
With twice the force an earthquake has, I gently closed the door.
The men knelt down before me; their intent I could not tell,
But then, upon me, through the window, morning sunlight fell.
We talked a while. I bravely uttered: "When you both withdraw,
May I, as Queen, request a thing I've never had before?"
They smiled and said, "Your Majesty has just to make it known."
"Well, might I have a little time — perhaps one hour — alone?"
The crown had set me free, then Albert made my heart content.
On him I lavished all the love thus far I had not spent.
When Albert died, I lived a sad recluse in mourning dress,
But Britain and the Empire grew to love me nonetheless.

71

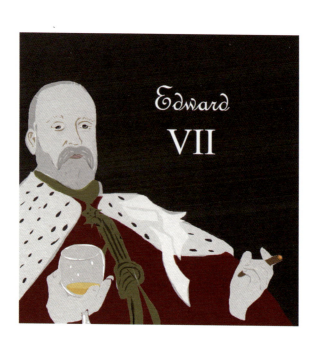

Edward

VII

Edward VII

(1901–1910)

I had a racy, raucous youth as Queen Victoria's heir;
My lifestyle drove my prim and proper parents to despair.
The Queen believed my personal deficiencies so great
She banned me from participating in affairs of state.
This forced me into idleness — her scheme thus only served
To push me to the life from which she wanted me preserved.
A connoisseur of wine, food, women, horse racing and cars,
And, yes, I liked a wager over brandy and cigars,
I wasn't just a playboy though; when called onto the stage
Of kingship, my warm manner thawed the stiff Victorian age.
Our splendid isolation from all Europe had to end,
And thanks to my diplomacy now France was Britain's friend.
The *Entente Cordiale* was really peace designed for war,
For who knows what a brand-new century might hold in store?
That I did make a decent king I hope my mother knows.
The throne's a more accommodating place than some suppose.

George
V

George V
(1910–1936)

The Navy taught me ships for stormy waters must be ready.
No reign has proved more turbulent; no king has proved more steady.
The First World War opposed three men who shared a grandmamma:
Myself (King George), the German Kaiser and the Russian Tsar.

When Germany struck Europe, with her systematic rage,
We needed help; thank God then our Dominions came of age.
They offered brave assistance in their Motherland's grim task,
And did not stoop to humble us by forcing us to ask.

A mix of anger, pride, eternal gratitude and shame
I lived with, for the million men who perished in my name.
Then Ireland was partitioned, and a General Strike then struck.
It seemed as if the fabric of the realm had come unstuck.
All I could do was press for peace and reason. By and by
The strain of kingship dulled the boyish twinkle in my eye.
The power of the ancients modern kings do not possess;
Believe me though — this doesn't make the burden any less.

75

Edward

VIII

Edward VIII
(1936)

You'll see I only reigned one year, and yet my life was long,

And I was very popular. Here's where it all went wrong:

I loved a woman who'd already worn a wedding ring,

So had to be a crownless husband, or a wifeless king.

My lone heart simpered louder than the Empire's chorus-roar:

I'd marry. Empire would survive. King Edward was no more.

Now then, as Britain tottered on another world war's brink,

My flirting with the enemy made Winston Churchill think:

"We'll have to send him somewhere where his actions cannot harm us."

Before I knew it I was sent to govern the Bahamas.

I thought I'd lead a prince's life, once peace had conquered war.

In fact my kingdom would not even let me back ashore.

A banished king, I lived in France with no-one but my wife.

So there you have it; time to reach a verdict on my life:

Romantic hero, not afraid to have his love revealed?

Or man who, fearing duty, used a woman as a shield?

George VI
(1936–1952)

A dutiful and humble prince, I wore my brother's crown,

Appalled by his rejection of so prized a hand-me-down.

As Duke of York I met a girl: Elizabeth Bowes-Lyon.

I took her hand; soft velvet glove containing fist of iron.

Her Grace when she was Duchess put a smile on every brow;

Her Majesty as Queen made men feel privileged to bow.

Together we would satisfy the public's greedy eye,

But just as we grew comfortable the world was shaken by

Another war: as night fell bombs fell, then the following day

I'd stand with the survivors where their homes once stood. Some say

No Emperor housed royally in palaces august

Has ever looked as dignified as I did in the dust.

In February nineteen fifty-two, the icy air felt thin.

My cancer-ridden lungs breathed out, and didn't breathe back in;

Meanwhile in Kenya, high up in the tree-tops, free of care,

A young, dark-haired princess inhaled the warm, late-summer air.

Elizabeth II

Elizabeth II
(1952–) *2022*

A slender figure dressed in black, I stepped down from the plane

To face, before my grief, the obligations of my reign.

On television sets the ancient ritual was shown:

Steady of foot and clear of voice I claimed my father's throne.

The Age of Empire autumned, but no Fall of Rome for us;

I lent much needed dignity to hasty exodus.

Now still, though Britain's dominance has long been at a close,

I'm head of sixteen states; I can content myself with those.

I serve quite unreservedly but ration what's on view.

I show the world two smiling eyes that no-one can see through;

Arrive, perform, then leave the stage, and offer no encore.

My royalty conserves itself, at length to offer more.

Now horse-riding I love, which puts my courtiers in fits;

They urge me down, imagining the royal skull in bits,

And tell me how the Conqueror was flung from where he sat.

I thank them with a nod, then I ride on, without a hat.

81

Sam Norman learned some things at
Neston County High School on the Wirral,
and then learned a few more at New College, Oxford.
He now lives in the Lake District, where he enjoys
playing squash, bridge and the piano.

Maria Smedstad grew up in Sundsvall, Sweden
before moving to England in 1994.
She gained a 1st class degree in Illustration in 2001
and now works as an illustrator, cartoonist and
writer from her Southampton studio.